P9-CQY-204

Pyaasa
Letters to my Grandma

Anusree Roy

Playwrights Canada Press
Toronto

Pyaasa & Letters to my Grandma © 2010 Anusree Roy
Introduction © 2010 Thomas Morgan Jones

PLAYWRIGHTS CANADA PRESS
202-269 Richmond St. W., Toronto, ON M5V IXI
416.703.0013 • info@playwrightscanada.com • www.playwrightscanada.com

No part of this book may be reproduced, downloaded, or used in any form or by any means without the prior written permission of the publisher, except for excerpts in a review or by a licence from Access Copyright, www.accesscopyright.ca.

For professional or amateur production rights, please contact the publisher.

We acknowledge the financial support of the Canada Council for the Arts, the Ontario Arts Council (OAC)—an agency of the Government of Ontario, which last year funded 1,681 individual artists and 1,125 organizations in 216 communities across Ontario for a total of $52.8 million—the Ontario Media Development Corporation, and the Government of Canada through the Canada Book Fund for our publishing activities.

Cover photo by Aviva Armour-Ostroff
Cover design by BFdesign
Type design by Blake Sproule

LIBRARY AND ARCHIVES CANADA CATALOGUING IN PUBLICATION
Roy, Anusree
Pyaasa & Letters to my grandma / Anusree Roy.

Plays.
ISBN 978-0-88754-911-3

I. Title. II. Title: Letters to my grandma.

PS8635.O898P93 2010   C812'.6   C2010-901156-2

First edition: April 2010. Second printing: October 2013.
Printed and bound in Canada by Imprimerie Gauvin, Gatineau.

This book is dedicated to Ma, Baba, and Didi,
for surviving 147-8th Street

To Thom and Dave,
thank you for being my brothers and co-creators

INTRODUCTION

Anusree Roy writes plays because she truly believes that they have the power to change the world.

This belief is contagious for both artists and audiences, and it is at the heart of each of her plays. As a participant in the development of both of these scripts, I have marvelled at the depth of Anusree's ability to capture the joy, pain, and horror of her characters' lives and relationships. Her courageous writing never shies away from darkness, misery, and violence, but always finds the humanity (and often the humour) at the core of each of her elements and themes.

Both *Pyaasa* and *Letters to my Grandma* are deeply rooted, whether set in Canada or India, in Anusree's Indian culture and Hindu faith. Her culture and religion help shape the world(s), the stakes, and the interactions of her plays. While writing and creating, she will often be heard saying of each character and each situation, "It would just have to be this way for them. It would *have* to be." Cultural influences aside, what makes each of her characters so accessible is what makes Anusree so engaging and beautiful as an artist, a colleague, and a friend: her honesty. It is the simple honesty within the writing of each character that brings them to effervescent life and imbues every word, every beat, and every silence with a crushing dramatic weight that is a joy to read and an honour to rehearse.

This is how she creates the empathy necessary for change. In *Pyaasa*, Meera's undying love for her daughter leads her to an action that ultimately crushes Chaya's future happiness, but she honestly could not have acted differently. In *Letters to my Grandma*, Amma's act of violence and deception to save her child was made as she decided there was nothing she would not do to save her newborn child. These moments make us question not only the characters' actions, but also the world that forces these characters to take these actions. We are forced to ask ourselves what we would have, or could have, done differently.

Following each performance, audience members were compelled to speak with Anusree. They wanted to share *their* stories and *their* personal experiences. *Letters to my Grandma* moved audiences to offer stories about their grandparents, about racism in their own families, and about their own families' experiences with war. There was one instance, following a performance of *Pyaasa*, where a woman admitted that she had spit on one of her untouchable servant's face while living in India, and tearfully asked Anusree for her forgiveness. Each conversation with each stranger spoke to a deep and meaningful connection they had made with the writing. It was as if the writing invited the audiences into Anusree's world(s) while allowing them to access new perspectives on their own lives.

My initial and immediate reaction to both scripts was the same as for many audience members. When Anusree read me the first half of *Pyaasa* after our initial meeting, I vividly remember bursting out of my seat, saying, "Where is the rest!" I was so viscerally connected to Chaya's journey that I found myself completely invested in knowing how the world she lived in would affect her future. Less than a year ago, when Anusree completed the newest rewrite of *Letters to my Grandma*, I read the last word alone (she had emailed me the text) and suddenly awoke to the understanding that everywhere I go and everything I do, those whom I love are with me, and affected by the decisions I make. The honour and privilege of being a part of the process of these plays' creation has been one of self-discovery for myself, the same self-discovery that I have seen in every audience.

In describing her culture, Anusree once explained to me that, "In Canada we think with our heads when we make decisions and our hearts when we feel decisions. In India we think and feel with our stomachs." To feed is of paramount importance, and the metaphor of feeding relates to all aspects of life, from faith to ambition to hatred and to love. With *Pyaasa* and *Letters to my Grandma*, Anusree feeds our minds, our hearts, our souls, and fills us with the hope that theatre really can change the world.

Thomas Morgan Jones

Pyaasa

This play is a solo play, it was written and intended for a single actor to play all roles. The play should be performed without an interval, with a running time of approximately forty minutes.

Pyaasa was first produced by Theatre Jones Roy at Theatre Passe Muraille, Toronto, between September 25 and 30, 2007 with the following company:

Anusree Roy: Playwright / Performer
Thomas Morgan Jones: Director / Dramaturg
David DeGrow: Lighting Designer / Stage Manager
Evan Ayotte: Costume Painter
Ryan McDougall: Technician
Aimee Nishtoba: Poster Design

Pyaasa is set in present day Bengal, India.

CHARACTERS

Chaya: Eleven years old. She is bright, filled with energy and has tremendous determination. She is hopeful for the future.

Meera: Mid-forties. She is very shrewd, very strict with her daughter, and fully understands how to use her social disadvantage to her advantage. She is plagued with lower-back pain.

Kamala: Mid-forties. She is confident, incredibly manipulative, and enjoys holding power over the lower castes.

Mr. Bikash: Mid-fifties. He is a rich, educated, and stern man. He loathes the untouchables.

Mr. Bikash's Home

Lights gradually come up on stage. MEERA is sitting crouched on the floor. She watches KAMALA come from stage right as she starts speaking in Bengali.

MEERA

Oh didi! Kamon aacho didi? Mone hocche koto din tomake dhekhi na didi... saree ta ki bhalo lagche tomake! Notun shari naki? Na didi, aami kicchu dhori ne. Chup kore boshe aachie... dhako balti-o-okhane aache. Na didi chui ne.[1] *(She gets up.)*

No didi. You didn't give soap no, so I didn't put. Bishash koro didi... Kothai dile shaban

---

[1] Oh sister! How are you sister? Feels like I haven't seen you in so long sister... your saree looks amazing! Is it new? No sister, I haven't touched anything. I have been sitting here real quiet... look, the bucket is right there. No sister I didn't touch it.

bolo?[2] I wait here every day didi, until you come, turn the tap on and then I go in. When have I ever touched anything in this house? I would rather die, jump off a bridge, be killed by a bus, set fire to my own tent, didi, before I would touch anything. No didi, I didn't touch it. I swear on my child.

MEERA touches KAMALA's hand on the word "child."

KAMALA   What are you doing... ki korcho ta ki?[3] Uff. Now your shadow fall on me, now I have to go take another shower. When will you people learn? You people come from somewhere and then chew my head. There is little food for your daughter, underneath the sink, take it before you leave.

MEERA   Thank you so much didi. You are so kind. Jano, didi, tomake ki jigesha korbo bhabchilam...[4] Is your boy still running the tea stall?

KAMALA   Ha kano?[5] Why you want to know?

MEERA   Na, didi... bhabchilam,[6] if you can please talk to him. Ahh ha, didi, oeirokom kore

---

2 Believe me, sister... When did you give me soap?
3 What are you doing?
4 You know what I was thinking of asking you...
5 Yes, why?
6 No, sister... I was thinking

dhekhcho kano?[7] Chaya is getting old no and she has no job. Today she has no job, tomorrow she will have no food to eat, and the next day she will be eating from the garbage. The next thing you know some street vendors will be coming and cutting off her hand and she will be sitting there, beside the streets, with a little begging bowl; begging, begging, begging, nobody is even listening to her, nobody is even giving her one *paisa* didi. The next thing you know, there will be some flies buzzing around some wound in her eye and then she will be losing one eye didi. No didi, that I cannot take. She cannot be losing one eye when she will already be having no hand. So, if she can come and clean all the teacups in your son's tea stall, that would be good, no? Whatever your son can pay...

KAMALA Ummmm... *Moree na.* Ahh ha.[8] Tea stall! You have some guts to you, na? Coming here and asking me to give your Chaya a job? *Aacha,*[9] Meera, tell me something, why you are forgetting that you are untouchable caste? Now your shadow fall on me, now I have to go to the Holy River to wash myself!

---

7 Ahh ha, sister, why are you looking at me like that?
8 An Indian expression of disgust.
9 Okay.

Ungrateful. I give her food to eat, is that not enough? The more we give your caste the more you want. Do you know what would happen if Sir Ji found out that I give you all their leftover food...? All you do is talk talk talk... you are lucky that I let you even talk to me. All the untouchables in your *basti* are scared to even look at me. I am the head servant of this house... not an untouchable like you.

What hand cut off? There will be no hand cut off... you have not changed one bit since I have known you. Hand cut off. Kotha theke je tumi eai gulpo gulo pao na ta aami aar ki bolbo.[10]

MEERA   Na, didi.[11] I didn't mean it that way didi. How long you have known me didi? Why you are saying things like that? Okay okay... your son does not even have to pay Chaya for the first two months, she will just sit there and clean. Tell him to give her some tea some time. She is loving tea, didi. Actually, come to think of it, she has never even tried tea, so that would be good beverage, no? Incentive to go to work. See didi, I save your son some

---

10 Not sure where you get all these stories from.
11 No, sister.

money didi. I am always thinking of you didi. Shob shomai tomar kotha chinta korchie.[12]

KAMALA Ummm… koto jano chinta… chini na jano aami tomake.[13] Okay. Okay. Now get back to your sweeping.

Eaai,[14] my husband brought fresh cow dung from the dump, you come to my house tonight and make those cow-dung cakes… I told you about this a week ago… he needs fresh cow-dung cakes to sell in the market next week. You come and I will give you some stale roti I save for your daughter.

And don't just come prancing around inside the house, wait outside, I will bring it to you.

MEERA Oh didi, yes then? So didi, yes then? I will send Chaya to work tomorrow morning didi. Tell your son she is a very good girl, will not touch anything. Nothing at all… all they have to do is bring the teacups to her, and she will wash them very well. God will bless didi!

---

12 I am constantly thinking for you.
13 Ummm… so many thoughts… as if I don't know you.
14 An Indian expression of calling someone without proper respect.

MMMMM. Look at her, thinks she is *maharani*.[15] Wait till Sir Ji comes and then she will know... servant like me. Joto shob. Neeje ke je ki mone kore na shae aami aare ki bolbo?[16]

> *MEERA makes one swift turn and walks upstage right and transforms into CHAYA, who is eating the leftovers from a bowl in her hand. She gradually makes her way to downstage centre.*

---

15 The queen.
16 Nonsense, what does she think of herself?

SCENE TWO
Meera's Home

CHAYA

Ummm ummm. Ma, Ma, Ma, I liking it very much. Ammar khhob bhalo lagche.[17] Can I have some more? *Jano*, Ma, there is something different in it today.

MEERA

And what is there to be different Chaya? Every day you drink boiled rice water. Now hurry up, your father will be back from the police station soon. I don't want him to see you standing around doing nothing. *(indicating to the bucket nearby)*

And... look at THAT bucket. It is filled with water already. *(Looks up at the tent and finds a hole in it. She walks up to the spot.)* God knows when they will fix this bridge. Every day they say,

---

17 I really like it.

today today today, and nothing is ever done. I don't think that they think people living underneath this bridge are even alive. Chaya, be a doll and go dump the bucket out... my back is hurting from sitting and making all those cow-dung cakes. Uff.

Walks towards stage left and transforms into CHAYA, *who walks towards the bucket placed stage right. Takes the bucket filled with water and disposes of it off stage right. Laughter/giggle can be heard offstage.* CHAYA *comes back in with the empty bucket and places it stage right. She realizes she has misplaced the bucket and corrects its placement. She runs towards her mother, hesitates, and then speaks.*

CHAYA   Ma, Ma, Ma, today morning when I went by English school the Nun Sisters were handing out free times-table books, I took two, Ma... they are not that hard. They only go up to about five... *(pauses) Hih?*[18] Kano Ma kano. Na na na... Ma, please. Aami chai na kaj korte. Kano?[19] You told me that I could go to school when I was ten, I'm eleven now. *(walks forming a semicircle from upstage left to upstage right and stands upstage right)* But this is not fair. Why? Didn't Kamala Aunty say that she

---

18 What?
19 I don't want to work. Why?

would give you all her son's old books if you made cow-dung cakes for her? Then? You always do that for her... why doesn't she give you books? *(walks centre stage)* You know what I forgot to say? *(sits)* Yesterday morning when I was coming back after picking up empty cans the Murialla man said that his daughter just passed class eight from an English school and and and he said that he would give me all her old books. So when I go to class eight, you don't have to buy me books, I will have them already. *(gradually moves stage left while seated)* See see see, Ma. Isn't that a good thing? You want me to make tea Ma? What if I burn myself...? Then nobody will be wanting to marry me and I have to sit at home all day.

> *CHAYA physically transforms into MEERA and gets up with great effort, walks stage left, and speaks to CHAYA who is sitting centre stage.*

MEERA

Chaya, ekdom chup koro. Ekdom mook bondo koro.[20] All this education will be getting you nowhere.

You think somebody will be wanting to marry you? Then they will come and tell me that you have too much education and you will

---

20 Keep quiet. Keep your mouth absolutely shut.

be sitting at home for the rest of your life. Just like Shampa's daughter. It is all Shampa's fault, who told her to put her daughter in English school. Now look at her, she is fourteen, fatherless, and not a single person wants to marry her. Plus, Kamala said that her son thinks that you will work very hard and he will give you tea some time. See tea, you have never been having tea before. Now you can go tell all your friends that you have been having tea before they do. Muk gomra korle cholbe bol.[21] Don't make that face; see how hard your father has to work cleaning the toilets in the police station? Chaya don't look at me like that. Chaya, don't make that face!

> MEERA *physically transforms into* CHAYA *and walks towards stage left on a sharp angle, turning around to face* MEERA.

CHAYA   I don't want to go. It's not my fault that they think that they can't touch us so all we have to do is sit there. I should have been born into Mr. Bikash's house, his daughter gets to touch everything because they are higher caste than us. Don't touch this… don't touch that… don't do this, don't do that, ahhhh. *(She crosses her arms facing the audience. Beat. Feels*

---

21 There is no point in making that face.

MEERA touch her left arm.) Fiiinnnneeee. When do I have to start?

MEERA   Five thirty tomorrow morning, I will wake you up. We can both get dressed together and then you can help me cook. Then, after work, we can go to the community well to get some water.

Community Water Line

MEERA smiles, picks up the bucket, and looks at CHAYA. She turns and physically transforms into CHAYA. They both walk upstage. They are now standing in line to get water at the community well. The line keeps moving through this scene.

CHAYA

(walking) Na, Ma... That was wrong. I'm going to try again, okay? *(takes position in line)* Two times one is two, two times two is four, two times three is six, two times four is NINE, two times five is... Uff ho Ma, you're not catching my mistake. When I said nine that was wrong... *(CHAYA physically transforms into MEERA and takes one step forward.)*

MEERA

Move with the line no Chaya. *(notices her friend Shampa at a distance and waves)* Ohh *aarre*

aarre[22] Shampa. Ki khobor... koto din tomar shate dhaka hoy na. Shob khobor thik aache? Bhalo?[23] How is your daughter doing? Any news on the marriage proposal? Na, na. Meyer shate ashechie[24] to get some water from the well. I should have come last night, look at this lineup. Every day it is getting longer and longer. Guaranteed those basti people are coming and stealing our water. Theirs is not fixed, no! No, it is still not fixed... all the basti people have been lining up in the government office for so long. Aarre move the line no, man... a little bit faster... I have to go home and wash utensils.

MEERA moves forward in line and indicates CHAYA to keep moving.

So as I say, I hear every month government inspector comes, looks at it and goes away. Nothing is ever done. I am sure they come to our well to steal our water. Thieves!

MEERA moves forward in line and indicates CHAYA to keep moving.

---

22 An Indian expression to draw attention.
23 Anything new? I haven't seen you in so long. How is everything? Well?
24 With my daughter here.

Aacha, do you know anything about the bridge being fixed? Ki mushkil boloto,[25] there is water all over my tent plastic.

Yes, we are still living there... last year my husband was going to build us a mud house, but it is so expensive, no? Also, my sister built one. The tin door cost her so much money... but this monsoon season, the entire thing collapse due to rain. She cried so much. AND THIS LINE IS NOT EVEN MOVING! All I want is a good tent plastic. But all government will give us is torn blue plastic? They might as well give us paper from now, we can only take newspaper and put on our roof and it will leak anyway. You only tell me, what is the difference between torn blue plastic and newspaper? The next thing you know, they will be coming and living underneath our tent with us and eating our food... which, come to think of it, will be a good thing. They need to see how we live and what we never eat! *(laughs)* Can you imagine... if they came and we gave them boiled rice water? *(chuckles)*

Ha? Yes, my husband? He is doing very well. Yes, he is becoming permanent now. They all love him very much. No, same pay as last time, every year they say they will give him

---

25 This is so much trouble.

more money. But this year it is for sure happening. I am having good feeling about it... and when it does, we will build a house with a tin door.

CHAYA Ma, *chalo na.*[26]

MEERA (*Annoyed by the interruption, she gives a sharp look to* CHAYA *and turns back to realize Shampa has left.*) Okay okay Shampa. I will see you later. Bye bye.

(*turns to look at* CHAYA) Chaya, when I am talking don't talk in the middle. She must have felt insulted by you. And this line is not even moving!

(*notices Kamala's son downstage left*) LOOK. Kamala's son. Chaya, don't look at him like that. He is higher caste than us, so don't even have any ideas. Now you are looking at him, the next thing you know he is touching your face and the next thing you know he is buying you bangles and the next thing you know you are having his babies! You are working for him now. Move eye, move eye.

CHAYA Na Ma, I am not even looking at him. Can I try my tables again?

---

26 Ma, let's go.

MEERA   Tables, tables, tables, how much will your tables help you when you're sitting there washing all those teacups?

(Suddenly racing towards downstage left. Speaking to Kamala's son.) Aaaaiiieee... Na na na na na na na we have been waiting in line. Jao pechone jao.[27] Go to the back of the line. We have been waiting in line far longer than you. And which basti you are from? No! We are from the bridge basti and this is our tap... you have to have your own tap, you cannot come here and steal our water. Now you are stealing our water, the next thing you say that the pump is yours and the next thing you say is that you will be coming and living underneath the bridge with us, the next thing you say that you want our food and our daughters too! I know your kind very well. What you think, we have no brain? We understand all. So, don't come here and do your *chalaki*.[28] Go along. Go! My husband works at the police station, you give me problem and he will send police after you!

---

27 Go to the back.
28 Chalaki is a Bengali word that could mean "to pull a fast one," depending on the context.

Kamala's son spits on her face. In a sharp turn she turns her face downstage right. She touches her face with her right hand to remove spit.

Aamar mukheo thutu fello![29] He spit on me! Come on, come move the line.

Storms off to join the line again. She takes position in line as CHAYA.

CHAYA

(looking upstage left) Ma. Why do you go to argue with them?

MEERA

They will turn the tap off in the next two hours and some people need it more than he does. But don't worry Chaya, one day my shadow will fall on him, and then he will know.

---

29 You spit on my face!

SCENE FOUR
Tea Stall

MEERA physically transforms into CHAYA. She walks downstage centre and sits. She takes tea glasses from the floor and wipes them (glasses should be mimed). On the second and third glass she spits and then wipes them. Laughs hysterically. Suddenly notices Kamala's son stage right and gets up, looking down.

CHAYA   Ha... hello. See, these teacups are almost clean and I have one more hour to go. *(pause)*

No I cannot look at you...

(turns left on the spot) No. My ma said that I cannot look at anyone that is higher caste than us. So... umm... I cannot look.

(*quickly walks downstage left and stands*) No no no no no no please don't make me look. My ma said that if I look at you, then you will go tell that we people look. Then my father will lose his job, he is a toilet cleaner in a lot of the police stations in this area, and then my mother will lose her job. She is a toilet cleaner in a lot of the houses... so, I cannot look. Yes... but.

> *In a sharp move she covers her eyes with her palms. Slowly she turns to face Kamala's son with her eyes still covered.*

Nooooooo, I will get in trouble. My ma said that I have to come here and clean all the tea-cups so I can get some tea, she doesn't have enough money for me for lunch... yes... but.

> *Gradually she uncovers her face and turns her head stage right, and then her body turns stage right (still on spot), she cups her hand and takes biscuits from Kamala's son in an "untouchable" manner. She smiles and looks at the food. She feels him watch her eat. She turns and starts to gobble her food. She picks up the last piece and looks at it. She physically transforms into MR. BIKASH who is also looking at the piece of food. She walks downstage centre and throws the food away.*

Mr. Bikash's Home

MR. BIKASH Kamala? Kamala. *(turns and snaps)*

Stand here. Have you been giving the toilet cleaner food? *(pause)* Answer me? *(pause)* Do not make me repeat the question.

KAMALA Na na, Sir Ji. I didn't do anything wrong. That toilet cleaner Meera said that if I didn't give her some food she would take her dirty hands and put it all over your house. So I got scared, Sir Ji, and gave her some food. But don't worry, nothing fresh. All the uneaten from your plate I gave her.

MR. BIKASH Where does she live?

KAMALA Underneath the bridge they have a tent. She lives there.

MR. BIKASH	Go tell her that she is no longer to work for me. I don't need her anymore. Bloody ungrateful bloodsucking untouchables. Dogs should eat them all! I give her place to work and she is stealing my food.
	Now go! What are you waiting here for?
KAMALA	Na na, Sir Ji, she is very poor, Sir Ji.
MR. BIKASH	Kamala, tell me one thing. Do you like your job here?
KAMALA	Yes, Sir Ji. No problem, I will go tell her that she is no longer to work for you.

SCENE SIX
Outside Meera's Home

KAMALA physically transforms into CHAYA who is skipping and who suddenly stops when she reaches stage left. She notices KAMALA.

CHAYA

Oh, hello. Yes. Yes, I know you. My ma and you work at the same house, right? I work at your son's tea stall. Did you know that? Yesterday, he gave me a tea biscuit and... *(She listens.)* What? Why? Did I do something wrong? But Ma said that she can't lose her job, then we will have to drink boiled rice water all the time. No... please tell them not to fire her! What did she do?

She realizes that KAMALA has left. Beat. She contemplates and enters her house running.

Ma Ma Ma Ma Ma, guess what I just found out... okay. So hear this. From now on I will work full time... like, like how you say? Like permanent, in the tea stall. And and and... he said that he would give me two tea biscuits... See, see, Ma, isn't that a good thing? If I went to school, I would probably not even do well and who needs school when I can learn how to make tea and cook. I can help you now. I promise, Ma, I will not even think of school anymore. All my times tables, I will not even say them anymore, Ma, I will not even bother you anymore, Ma, because I know that it is a waste of my time. And, when he starts to pay me, I can run the family. I can buy food and you won't even have to make cow-dung cakes for Kamala Aunty. You can just sit at home and rest.

Beat. Contemplates and then speaks.

Okay, in other news, I just met Kamala Aunty outside. She said that you don't have to go to your job anymore because they don't want you anymore.

She didn't say why.

But don't worry, Ma. I will work from now. So you can sit at home and rest. See see, Ma... isn't that a good thing?

MEERA   Chaya, ekdom muk bondo Koro.[30] "I can run the family"! How old are you? Go wash your face and bring a bucket. The tent plastic is leaking again. Put it right there. There is little boiled rice water in the pot, drink it. Put some salt in it to bring the flavour. *(watches CHAYA walk and sit downstage right)* Has crying ever changed anything? Look at me! *(pause)* No. Then swallow your tears, I don't want to see them anymore.

---

30 Close your mouth.

Right Outside Meera's Home

MEERA physically transforms into CHAYA. CHAYA turns to check if anyone is watching, she picks up the bucket and sits with it, placing it front stage centre. She takes out a Kajol container (eye makeup) hidden in the folds of her saree and applies it. She undoes her braid. She checks her makeup and hair in the reflection of the water in the bucket. During this process she constantly looks back to check if anyone is watching. She dips her hand in the water and drinks. She looks up and speaks to God.

CHAYA   The tea-stall boy gave it to me... don't tell Ma. He is higher caste than us. She will break my bones with a bat.

Hears MEERA call her offstage.

Ha, aaschie.[31]

Aaschie. Aaschie.

> *Picks up the bucket and walks two steps back. Places the bucket down and pays salutation to God.*

Aaschie.

> *Says "aashchie" as she keeps walking backwards. Places the bucket upstage and is now in the next tea stall. She accepts tea.*

---

31 Yes, coming.

SCENE EIGHT
Tea Stall

She speaks nervously as she holds her tea glass. She is speaking to Kamala's son.

CHAYA

Did you know that this is my first cup of tea? Ever. Nooo I have never been having tea before. And now you are so sweet to making me tea. It is sweet tea, right? *(takes a sip)* Oh... it's so hot... but I liking it very much. My ma says that all rich people drink tea at four o'clock in the evening... I know it is not four o'clock in the evening, but I feel like a rich people.

Did you know that my ma thinks that I am at my friend's house... yes, Durga, she works here. My ma doesn't know I am working here this late... it's ten o'clock... she will get very angry. *(Surprised, she feels the tea-stall boy trying to touch her. She walks two steps forward.)* Here, my tea is done.

No, please don't touch me again. I have to go now. *(feels his touch again and takes two steps forward)* Ma aamake boleche tomar shate beshi kotha na bolte. Aami tomar jonno kaj korte aachis. Ha, I shotti bolchi.[32] Ma tells me this all the time. I only come to work here. You told me if I work till ten you will give me two tea biscuits. Well you should give them to me now. *(Shocked, she turns to face the tea-stall boy stage right.)* What? Why? I have to keep working here. You cannot fire me like that.

> *She hurries downstage.*

No... please don't touch me again.

No, my mother will get very angry.

I don't want any more tea... I am leaving now.

> *She is raped by the tea-stall boy. This segment is executed only through CHAYA's breath and gesture. NO rape screams.*

---

32 Ma told he not to talk to you. I only come to work for you. Yes, I am telling you the truth.

Lighting note: The rape should take place in a tight box of light created by a top light.

Sharp inhale—hand apart to indicate the teacup dropping.

Inhale from mouth—chin on left shoulder. Exhale.

Inhale—chin on chest right. Exhale.

Inhale—right hand on left breast. Exhale.

Inhale—left hand on inner right thigh. Exhale.

Inhale. Both hands on chest and looks upstage left.

She is now at the police station being interrogated.

The interrogator stands downstage left to create the police officer.

No nooo. *(looks upstage right)*

I was having tea. No. I didn't steal it. He made it for me and gave me tea.

It's not my... *(looks downstage left)* sorry *(looks upstage right)*.

He wanted to touch my face.

(looks downstage left) I told him it was wrong though. *(looks upstage right)* Sorry.

No, he didn't listen.

Ten o'clock.

He told me if I worked till ten he would give me two tea biscuits and I wanted my ma to have two tea biscuits.

It's really not my fault. I told him to leave me alone. He didn't listen and I...

    Looks upstage left. Looks down. Pause.

Here. *(touches her lips)*

Here. *(touches her neck)*

Here. *(touches her left breast)*

    Touches her inner right thigh.

(big inhale) I didn't do anything. I didn't.

He forced me...

(looks upstage left) Why will you not help? *(looks downstage right)*

Sorry, but this is my life. My father works here, why will you not help?

> *Long pause. A moment's beat. She is now right outside the police station.*

Honour. Honour honour.

School school school.

No no no no no no no no no no no no no.

> *As she says her "nos" she starts walking and transforms into* MEERA, *who has just entered* MR. BIKASH's *house.*

MEERA   NO NO NO NO NO.

Kamala!

Kamala? Come down here right now. *(pause)*

I have been working here for years after years scrubbing this very floor and cleaning that toilet! *(pause)* I am never disrespecting you; I touch nothing! Always smiling. Always, always, always. Smiling I talk to you, smiling I come to your house to make YOUR cow-dung cakes and smiling I let your son not pay my daughter! And this is what he does?

Rascal.

> *Long pause. MEERA takes a deep breath. She removes her aachal (the part of her saree that goes over her chest) with her right hand and stands facing the audience. She takes the aachal and wipes each wall of MR. BIKASH's house while laughing hysterically. By doing this she has now soiled MR. BIKASH's house with her untouchable hands.*

SCENE NINE
MEERA'S HOME

She enters her house and notices CHAYA *on the floor sitting and crying. She pauses and remembers a story.*

MEERA

When your father saw you for the very first time he held you. The shadow of the moonlight was falling on your face. And he named you Chaya. Shadow. We both loved that name very much, because you were the only one. I think it is a good thing. Believe it or not, it's a good thing. *(She takes a step closer to* CHAYA.*)* Chaya, you are lucky that this man has agreed to marry you. These days it is very hard to find a husband, and that too, to find a husband for somebody that is used, is even harder. *(She takes a step closer to* CHAYA. *Pause.)* I know that he is very old but he will know what to do to make you happy. Plus, they are not asking for a lot of dowry Chaya... only three goats, one cow and some sarees. We can do that... we will manage that somehow. You will be happy. I am telling you. The best thing we can do for you is to get you married... but you have to make sure you have a son Chaya. That will take care of everything. Life is not easy, Chaya... but you have to believe in it.

> *MEERA takes out a container of vermilion from the folds of her saree and sits beside CHAYA.*

Today when this red vermilion will be touching your forehead you will be married... and you will be happy. I know that. This is for you Chaya.

> *MEERA slowly transforms into CHAYA. She watches her mother leave and mouths the word "Ma." Gradually she removes the lid of the container and places it stage left. She takes the red vermilion with her right hand and puts it on her forehead with her eyes closed. Her hand works its way down from her head to her neck. She makes two soft crying sounds and looks up at God.*

The End

Letters to my Grandma

This is a solo play, it was written and intended for a single actor to play all roles. The play should be performed without an interval, with a running time of approximately forty-five to fifty minutes.

This version of *Letters to my Grandma* was first produced by Theatre Passe Muraille, Toronto, between November 25 and December 12, 2009 with the following company:

Anusree Roy: Playwright / Performer
Thomas Morgan Jones: Director / Dramaturg
David DeGrow: Production Design
Dini Conte: Stage Manager
Developed by Theatre Jones Roy with the support of Theatre Passe Muraille

An earlier version of *Letters to my Grandma* was produced by Theatre Jones Roy with the support of Theatre Passe Muraille between March 3 and 8, 2009 with the following company:

Anusree Roy: Playwright / Performer
Thomas Morgan Jones: Director / Production Dramaturg
David DeGrow: Lighting and Sound Designer/Stage Manager
Thomas Morgan Jones and David DeGrow: Set Design
Judith Rudakoff, Andrew Cheng, Dawn Nearing, and Yvette Nolan: Dramaturgy

Letters to my Grandma is set during pre- and post-WWII in various places in and around India and Toronto, Canada.

CHARACTERS

Grandma (Young): A fighter, tremendously determined.

Grandma (Older): Has trouble breathing, which makes her inhale sharply through her mouth. She is very wise while also being completely set in her way of thinking. She visibly suffers from arthritis.

Malobee: Is full of love and fear. She is torn between loyalty to her family and her hope for happiness.

Ma: A strict and practical Indian mother.

Nurse: Knows her place in society and how to benefit from it. She has a sharp, nasal voice.

MALOBEE enters holding an Indian bridal plate.
She is singing the following Sanskrit mantra.

SCENE ONE

MALOBEE   Om niranjanam nityam anantarupam Bhaktanukampa dhrita vigraham vai, Ishavataram parameshamidyam Tam Ramakrishnam shirasha namamah.

Amma, today I am getting married aar tumi nai.[1] You are not here, kintu chinta koro na,[2] I brought all your letters with me. All of them. See, this is your last one. Still unopened.

I don't know how to open it. I am scared. I don't know how I am going to get married without your blessings. I need your blessings, Amma. I need you to have accepted this marriage. I wish you were in Toronto today. With

---

1 ...and you are not here.
2 But don't worry.

43

me. I try to find courage in thinking how it was for you to have gotten married when you were seventeen, surrounded by the war, four years younger than I am now. You must have had one of these also. Right? Flowers, thala,[3] ghonta...[4] but I bet you didn't have an unopened letter. No... no you didn't. I have an unopened letter, and you were dealing with the aftermath of the war...

The plate unexpectedly drops from her hands, resulting in a sharp sound along with its contents scattering on the floor. The actor transitions from MALOBEE *to her* GRANDMA, *when* GRANDMA *was eighteen during the war. She is holding her baby, panicking.*

---

3 Plate.
4 Bell.

SCENE TWO

GRANDMA

Bachao! Bachao! Kau ache! Aamar kache baby! Bachao! Shh...[5] someone will come for us. Shh. Stay calm. Ma is here. *(She spots a passerby.)* PLEASE! Please please. There was hatred in everyone's eyes. Everyone is dead... their eyes are dead. *(notices a passerby, runs towards them)* Dada,[6] dada, dada, where is everybody? I have a baby, only five hours old, dada, please help. Do you know where my family... No, dada, we are all Hindu. Our full blood is Hindu... not Muslim at all. What do you mean "Muslim Trucks"? They don't have Hindu trucks picking up Hindu people? Why not? But this is a Hindu area. Wait... wait... *(notices someone else, runs towards them)* Didi,[7] didi, didi, my husband has left me, didi... no... only a few hours old, didi. Do

---

5 Save me! Save me! Is anyone here! I have a baby! Save me! Shhh...
6 Brother.
7 Sister.

you know where the Basu family is hiding? Which ship? When did they leave? What... listen... come back... No they didn't. They couldn't have left. We will find them, shona.[8] You just stay alive... that's all you do. Ma will fix everything. Ma will be here. Always always always. Hai Thakur tumi dhekho... tumi![9]

> *Startled, she turns around to the sounds of a truck roaring by.*

Eh wait wait! STOP THE TRUCK! Stop the tuck. Please, I have a baby... save us. Bahisab... bhaisab.[10] Mai Muslim hoo.[11] I am a Muslim. Allah Ki kassma.[12] I swear on our Allah. Yeh mera baccha hai.[13] I just gave birth, bhaisab. Please bhaisab... you will be able to fit us in your truck. No I won't! I will sit on the floor. If you want I will not even breathe in there. Look look... that woman that you have in there, she is not even Muslim. No, that one, the one with the little girl child... Allah ki kassam. She is the nurse that used to work in the womens' ward. No she is not!

---

8 Sweetheart.
9 Dear God, you see us through, you!
10 An endearing term in Hindi used in reference to calling an unknown man brother.
11 I am Muslim.
12 I swear on Allah.
13 This is my child.

These Hindus are taking up our space. She is not Muslim... See... bhaisab, wouldn't you carry a Muslim and her baby so Allah blesses you? My family is very rich, you take me to the ship and my husband will give you money.

Get the nurse off. Get her off!

No no no, don't throw the child. Throw the mother. Throw her!

The woman is thrown off the Jeep. GRANDMA *spits on her.*

YOU ARE HINDU! What baby? See, these Hindus will come and make up stories. I don't know her. Allah ki kassam. Please, bhaishab, we are wasting time. The ship will leave soon and I have to find my husband so he can give you money.

She gets on the truck.

(She sits, speaking to the girl child.) Stop your crying. Your mother will be fine. Stop it.

Sudden pang of guilt. Beat. Looks around and speaks to the rest of people on the bus.

Are you all Muslim? Me neither. Will you pray with me for her? She was the Najma, the Muslim nurse who helped me deliver my baby.

She closes her eyes and prays.

SCENE THREE

MALOBEE is at Pearson International Airport in Toronto. She comes out of the bathroom, rushes to see her mother.

MALOBEE   Ma. You will not even believe. They have something called the automatic flush. You just stand there and it flushes...

MA   Malobee, your baba will be here any minute. Sit on the luggage or it'll get stolen.

MALOBEE   *(sits on a suitcase, contemplates)* Why does it have to rain? So irritating. I thought our first day in Toronto would be, I don't know, bright and sunny. *(notices Baba)* Oh, Baba is coming.

She gets up and listens to Baba.

Oh my God. What are we supposed to do now?

MA
What you mean he is not answering? How long will we wait in this rain?

MALOBEE
Check with the immigration desk, they might be able to help? *(Baba leaves.)* Wait, I'll come.

> MALOBEE *follows Baba in the immigration line They wait.*

Uff. Baba. Darao na. Aami toh kotha bolchie.[14]

> *She gets called forward by the immigration officer.*

Hello. I am fine, thank you, and how are you? Good. Umm... I was wondering if you could please help us. We just arrived in the BA99 flight and... hmm? No, BA99 from Calcutta, to Heathrow, to Toronto. And... Yes. No. No complaints. They were very nice to us. They gave us lunch and peanuts. *(awkward)* Yes. Yes we have our luggage. Oh, yes, the problem is that we have been waiting, for a very long time now. Yes, outside, and it's raining. No... we don't have any relatives here... but Malkit Singh, from the immigration company WWICS was going to pick us up and... oh WorldWide Immigration Consultancy Service. We will stay at their

---

14 Gosh. Dad. Wait. I will talk to him.

guest house for a month. Can you give them a call for us? ...Yes, my father tried but he is not answering... maybe if you call? *(beat)* Please, ma'am, we are new in Toronto and... Oh okay, can anyone else help? Oh. Okay. Good night to you too.

> MALOBEE *fakes a smile. They both turn to leave the airport.*

Mmmh, naka maye, sahajjo korte parlo na. Boshe toh aache oie khane.[15] Baba, I think we should take a taxi. Also, can we buy a phone card to call Amma? *(walks toward MA)* Ma, hurry hurry, we are taking a taxi.

> *They enter the guest house. She's amazed by the filth around her and stands still.*

Oh my God, why are we staying here?

MA   Malobee, don't complain.

MALOBEE   I am not complaining. It's so dark here and *(suddenly realizes)* are we sharing this room?

MA   Speak softly. The other guests will hear.

---

15 Mmmh, annoying lady, couldn't even help us. She is just sitting there.

MALOBEE	(*whisper*) But Baba promised that we would get our own guesthouse and I would get my OWN room. Where will I sleep?
MA	On that bed. It is only matter of a month.
MALOBEE	I cannot share one bed. I just cannot.
MA	Do you think I am enjoying this? Leaving my mother behind? Reduced to one single room? There is already enough problems with your amma back there. We are living out of six suitcases for a while and that's that.
MALOBEE	I hate it.
MA	Good. I have to call and let her know we have reached…
MALOBEE	No, I have the phone card. I'll call.
MA	Don't complain unnecessarily. She will worry otherwise.

> *MALOBEE sulks as she sits on the ground. She brings out the phone card and scratches the number.*

MALOBEE	Talk.

> *She audibly dials a ten-digit number starting with area code 416. Pause. She listens.*

English. *(pause)* One. *(pause)* What does press pound mean?

> *Pause. She audibly dials the* PIN *number from the calling card. Pause. She dials a fifteen-digit international area code starting with 0119133.*

Pound. *(pause)* Ah! Ringing. Hello. Is this Briddho[16] old home? I am calling long-distance from Canada... can you connect me to room 14C, please... yes, 14C... Yes, quickly please. *(pause)* Hello, Amma. Tumi kamon aacho?[17] Yes, we have reached safely... no it was on time. There were no problems at all. Yes he came to pick us... it is very beautiful here... Yes, they are very friendly. Yes... I like it... a lot. Tumi kamon aacho?[18] How is your nurse doing? What? What do you mean horrible? Give her some time, Amma. I am sure she is very nice. Did you take your Autrin today? Good. Make sure you take it once only, okay? Okay, now talk to Ma and I will talk to you later. Yes, Amma, I promise to write to you. Promise, promise, promise. There, I said it three times. Bhalo theko.[19] Here is Ma...

---

16 Old age.
17 How are you?
18 How are you?
19 Stay well.

SCENE FOUR

GRANDMA's room in Calcutta. She is in an old-age home with her NURSE, Shabnam, by her side.

GRANDMA

Nurse. Oie, nurse. What did you do to my slippers. Ha? You think I am not watching. I don't have eyes anymore? Because my daughter is now gone to foreign you will be robbing me and giving it to that dirty son of yours? Give me back my slippers right now, or I will cut that dirty Muslim head of yours.

NURSE

Aare aare aare,[20] na, dadi.[21] How many times will you cut my Muslim head? You are wearing your slippers already. And you be leaving my son alone. Why I go to be robbing you? Hai?[22]

---

20 A Hindi expression of being flustered.
21 Grandma in Hindi.
22 Why.

GRANDMA   Have they called? How long has it been?
            Why haven't they called?

NURSE   Aare, dadi. You sit now. So much thinking
            you are doing for them, now that they are
            in foreign. You should have gone with them
            to foreign land. Then no tension you will be
            having.

GRANDMA   Foreign land, foreign people and their for-
            eign talk. Heard enough of their foreign talk
            in my lifetime. I will die here in my mother
            soil. Shabnam, pick up the phone and see if
            the line is dead.

NURSE   Aare, dadi, I pick up just a little ago. Sit now,
            I will get your medicine.

GRANDMA   Don't argue with me. Go find my slippers.
            My feet are getting cold. If I see that dirty
            son of yours wearing them I will beat him
            so...

            The phone rings.

            Is that Malobee? Is she calling? Give the
            phone. Give na. *(She's given the phone.)* Move
            from here. Move na.

Heellllo, Malobee shona. Thik aachie.[23] You have reached safely? Was it late? Was there problem? Did the man come? Are they friendly? You like it? Ahe?[24] My nurse is horrible. My other nurse has left and now they have stuck me with a dirty Muslim nurse.

No, I am telling you, she is wearing my slippers. Hope your mother is happy now that she has stuck me in this hole.

I am telling you she is stealing my shoes. Disgusting! Yes. I am taking my Autrin. Okay. You will write to me? Promise?

---

23 Doing well.
24 What?

SCENE FIVE

One year later. MALOBEE *narrates a letter to her* GRANDMA.

MALOBEE   Sricharaneshu Amma, bhalo accho?[25] Dear Amma, how are you? I got your letter last week. That took quite a while, ha? Three weeks since you posted it. You have to start using the phone more often, Amma, then we can talk more. I know you are angry, but Ma has said it a hundred times, Baba's job change was not his fault.

Beat.

Anyway, today is the thirteenth, one full year in this new country, ha? Ki tara tari time flies, na?[26] Bishshashi ei hoy na,[27] that it was just

---

25 Respected Amma, are you well?
26 How quickly time flies, no?
27 I cannot even believe that ...

last year I wrote to you saying how much I hated the winter in Toronto. And now I can't wait for it to snow. It looks so beautiful outside. You can see the patterns of the flakes. Eai mone hoy kalkaye[28] we landed in the airport, cold and wet in the rain, somehow managing to sleep all four of us on that one bed. I still feel new though, still like an immigrant. I don't know when or how that will change, but I know for now it's still there.

Beat.

Anyway, I have a teacher here, Mrs. Hardy. She is Indian, married to a white man. It is totally acceptable here. Whites marry blacks, Indians marry Chinese, probably cows marry chicken! But they still make fun of me though, calling me Paki, so I guess they are not *that* accepting, but don't worry, all the people who call me that are not my friends anyway. And I think the next time someone calls me that I will call them an *American* and then they will get my point.

Beat.

So Mrs. Hardy gave us an assignment for OAC English class; I have to write about the most

---

28 It feels like yesterday...

influential person in my life, and of course I picked you. I have so many questions for you. Why didn't you tell me more about the war? Ma tells me these stories that you NEV-ER told me about. I don't even know what to ask. What was it like to be on that train with refugees? Ma said that Japan used to carpet bomb Burma and you had to steal from other people to eat? How did it feel when Dadai came back four years after the war, when you thought that he was dead and they made you wear widow's white. Did you hate him for that? All these years I have lived with you and now that I have moved far I am trying to get to know you. There is a lot of getting to know going on right now... there is a boy... he is nice. His name is Mark. I am getting to know him too.

I miss you, Amma. You and your stories. I love you so much. Please please please write to me. Bhalo theko, Bee.

PS Everyone here calls me Bee. Short form for Malobee. Pretty cool, na?

SCENE SIX

MALOBEE is now in her apartment with her mother.

MA   Again you are lying to me.

MALOBEE   I am *not* lying, Ma. It was one hockey game. One game. And Mark didn't even drive me home. I walked, I swear.

MA   How many times do you have to hear this? You are to not see this boy, Malobee. Baba and I are working very hard here for you not to be running around the boy. He is way too old for you and you will not disobey me.

MALOBEE   Ekata game chilo,[29] Ma, and Deepa was with us the whole time.

---

29 It was one game.

MA   Malobee, listen to me. I am telling you one thing now, and you will remember it. There are some things that are just impossible. I will not be hearing from my Indian friends here that my daughter is now happy with a loafer.[30]

MALOBEE   Do you not want me to be happy, Ma?

MA   Boka boka kotha bolo na![31] Find someone else to be happy with. And what do you think Amma would say? She will never forgive you for this nonsense. And when was the last time you called her? Boys, boys, boys, that is all that you are doing now! You are becoming completely Canadian!

MALOBEE   Please, Ma.

MA   No please! I am working very hard here to maintain Amma's health. You will not ruin it. You are running around the boy when Baba is working...

MALOBEE   *(frustrated)* Baba is working Baba is working Baba is working. That is all I have to hear now. He is here because he wanted that job.

---

30 In this context "loafer" means worthless.
31 Don't say foolish things!

For once, *I* am happy and making friends. Can you please be happy for me?

MA   Stop with the arguing! I don't want to hear about this anymore. And if it is okay with you, I am going to call my mother to see how she is doing. Ungrateful.

   MA stares for a beat.

SCENE SEVEN

MA transitions into GRANDMA. Her health is slightly worse than before.

GRANDMA

Your letters made me cry. They made me cry for so many reasons. You have asked so many questions to me for this class. Not sure where to start. Yes, I was seventeen when my father married me away. From wealth to middle class, I never argued. At eighteen I had my first baby; he left me the day before the delivery, I never argued. After what felt like years of starvation and hiding, the war ended in Burma. I came back from Burma to India with my little baby, and sat with the refugees on the ship. They touched me. I was a wealthy man's daughter, but I never for once argued. Things were even worse in India. The partition had created a special type of hatred between the Hindus and the Muslims. Everywhere you went you were asked what religion you were from. One wrong answer and you were stoned to death. We were told to hide everything. Bury them deep in the soil. Many women buried all their jewellery in the "field of gold," to come back and find them stolen. The only thing I wanted to save were my beautiful bangles...

Lights and sound indicate a time change. A riot can be heard in the background. GRANDMA stands and changes into her younger self during the partition war. She is panicked.

Oh my God!

She runs and grabs her baby, which is lying at stage left. She runs from stage left to stage right and notices a pile of bodies on the ground. She panics and runs upstage right. She places her baby on the floor, takes off her bangles, and buries them in the ground. She kisses the ground as a final goodbye to her bangles and freezes mid-kiss as she realizes a Muslim man is standing right beside her and her baby, pointing a gun in her face.

No. No I am not. I... I was saying my Namaz.[32] Doing my... my prayers and kissing the ground. You want me to say a prayer for you? I say a prayer for you. Ha?

---

32 Prayer (the formal prayer of Islam).

Says the prayer with the palms of her hand in front of her face.

Yaha Allah isko tu maaf kar. Isko tu zindagi ke har kushi deydey, mare Allah. Allah tujhe maaf kare.[33] *(finishes her prayer)* See, bhai, Allah will bless you and forgive your sins.

Ha? No, bhai, we are of the same kind. Look for someone Hindu, na, bhai. Why me and my child? We have nothing to give.

Beat.

Shukriya Bhaaisab. Allah rehem kare.[34]

She watches the person leave. She walks quickly. Stops. A Hindu man has approached her.

Na, dada, aami eaikhane thaki.[35] Shotti bolchie.[36] Ha?

Beat. Looks at her child. Beat.

No, not my child. She was just lying there, so I picked up. You want her? You can have—

---

33 Dear Allah you forgive him. Give him all the happiness of life, my Allah. May Allah forgive you.
34 Allah forgive you.
35 I live here.
36 I am saying the truth.

Offers her child over, explaining, trying to convince.

I don't want her either... see, see, look. Look at this belly. It is totally infected. Puss is coming out and she is crying all the time. Look, look here, totally green it is and her ear is also totally infection. It will fall off.

Beat.

Oh, I am keeping because I am hearing that childless mothers are trading for food. So keeping her for trading only. See, if you take her then you have to take care of her, na. Why take that headache on your head? Best you leave her with me, na?

Beat.

Dhonnobad, dada.[37] God will bless.

Watches them leave. She runs and sits on the ground downstage right. She picks up a piece of fabric and places it around her ear, as if wearing a hijab. She spits on her finger and puts the spit near her child's mouth to hydrate her.

---

37 Thank you, brother.

Water. Come on. Lick. Lick it. Good, my good daughter.

Shhhh... *(speaks to the baby quietly)* if they say, "Are you Hindu," nod. Okay? If they say, "Are you Muslim," nod. Just nod. Just keep nodding. They are what they are asking. Are you listening? I am going to put my hand over your mouth, okay? Don't be scared. Ma is going to be right here.

> *She puts her hand over her baby's mouth and rocks back and forth.*

Shhhh...

> *She looks startled, panicky. A Hindu woman comes in. She yanks her hijab off and shields her child from the intruder.*

Please please please! Don't! Don't take her! She is my only child I have. Please! Please! No, no food. Nothing at all. You... you... want gold? You want some gold? Go to the field of gold. You will find lots of gold there.

> *Beat.*

I swear I am saying truth! You walk past the cow shed and the little river. Then under the

gach[38] you will see the field. It is full of gold.
Buried in the soil. Hindu gold. Muslim gold.
I swear. Leave us alone…

Ha?

Beat.

Tell me what you are first.

Beat.

Hindu? I am Hindu too. I am too. Now leave
us alone? Go to the field. Go.

> *She watches the woman leave. She runs upstage
> right, places her baby, and digs out the bangles
> from the earth. She slowly puts her bangle on as
> she transforms into the old grandma. Old grand-
> ma sits on her bench and we are placed back in
> the old-age home.*

I thanked God many times that night that I
didn't hide my bangles in the field. Now all I
have are these bangles for you.

---

38 Tree.

Moment by moment, years passed. We starved all the time. The war making us bitter. The British making us hate each other.

In my mind, I kept thinking of that girl child in the truck.

Night after night, I wondered what happened. I am sure her mother Najma died that night in Ochin. Because of me she must have died. My beautiful village of Ochin was in flames that night.

I wondered if Allah would ever forgive me for throwing her off the truck. I wondered if Allah hated me.

SCENE EIGHT

GRANDMA changes to MALOBEE. Time has passed.

MALOBEE   I want you both to meet him.

MA   Proshnoi uthe na,[39] Malobee. Absolutely
       not. Tomake baar bar na kora hochay[40] to see
       him. Yet you do. On the sly. Regularly. It's the
       facts, Malobee. Just as simple as that. I have
       told you this before, there are some things
       that are very hard...

MALOBEE   You know what's hard, Ma? Its hard to be
           called a dirty Hindu. That's hard.

MA   I have lived my life, Malobee, aamar kichu
       na.[41] Think about Amma. Just once. What
       will this do to her her? Day after day it is be-

---

39 It's out of the question.
40 Repeatedly you are being told not to see him.
41 It doesn't matter to me.

70

coming impossible for that nurse to take care of her and she is throwing tantrums all the time. This news will break her. If you want to go ahead with this you will have to tell her yourself. You will have to make peace with her. Not me.

MALOBEE   I will. You meet him just once and I will do it. Aami Amma ke bojha bo.[42]

I promise promise promise.

Beat.

MA   Fine.

---

42   I will explain to her.

SCENE NINE

MALOBEE dials GRANDMA's phone number.

MALOBEE   Hello. Is this Briddho old home? Hi. Can you connect me to room 14c please? Thank you.

Waits with anticipation.

Hi Amma. Kamon aacho,[43] you are doing well? Good. You still taking your Autrin? Good, good—

Ahh... So, there is something I umm... wanted to say. Ahh... remember how last week I told you that I have a really good friend, Mark? Yes, Mark. Umm... well, I wanted to say that I really like him.

---

43   How are you?

Beat.

Like, he has become my special friend. He met Ma and Baba yesterday. Yes, for the first time. Well, they think he is okay. They want me to tell you first and...

Beat.

Yes, yes, yes *it is* a good thing, right? It is a good thing. That's what I am trying to tell them. Because I am getting older. *And...* No no, he is not British. He is *not* British. But, umm... what I wanted to say was that, he umm... he calls himself Mark, but that's not his real name. That's like a nickname, right? You know how I say that people here call me "Bee" from Malobee. Ya. Umm... his real name is... Mohammed. Mohammed Ahmed.

Yes. Yes, he is Muslim. Yes, from Pakistan. But, but... but they are really progressive. Like like like his family is really progressive. And and and they believe in in in Islam and they are really good people. You know how you used to always say that in the war there were dirty Hindus and then there were good Hindus? Same thing, but these are good Muslims, Amma, and you will really really like him if you got to know him... do you want talk to him someday? You could talk to him and...

GRANDMA has hung up.

Hello? Hello? Amma? Hello?

Shit.

(to herself as she redials the number) It's okay. It's okay.

Waits for connection.

Hello. Hi. My line got disconnected. Could you connect me to room 14C again, please. Thank you.

Pause.

Tell her it's her daughter calling and she really needs to talk to her.

Pause.

Please please. Just just give her the phone.

Put the phone near her ear, just one more time, please.

Pause.

Can you just please try.

NO NO, listen. Hello.

They hang up.

Shit. Shit. Shit. Shit. Shit.

SCENE TEN

MALOBEE transitions to GRANDMA. *She is weaker than before.*

GRANDMA   I will have one of you in my house. How they are saying yes. They are going to foreign and becoming foreign.

WHY I LIVE TO SEE THIS?

NURSE   Aare aare aare na, dadi. The way you are running, you will fall. And why didn't you tell her about sending me the extra money? Ha?

GRANDMA   They have left me here to die this way. That is what they are doing.

NURSE   Oh ho… You wanting to call her again? I can get you connection. Ha? Let us do that. Call her again and you talk to her. Remember, I am telling you, I am needing some extra money this month, na, so need to be asking that, na. My son needing some reading books for school, na.

GRANDMA   Always after stealing from me, you are still wanting more...

NURSE   I am never stealing from you. Aare, let me get you connection so we can both talk now. Ha.

GRANDMA   You are not even worthy of my feet and you are lying to my face. Dirty Muslim.

NURSE   (*trying to be patient*) Aare, dadi, listen to me. Khamokha[44] you are getting all angry. You hush now. I am making call for you. Listen, first let me be asking for the money. And then you can be telling her about dirty Muslim as long you like. Good plan!

GRANDMA   Leave. Go away now, Shabnam. Leave me...

NURSE   Oookaay. Leaving now. Finish up with all your crying. And when I am back, I will give you bath and then we will make call.

            NURSE *transitions to* GRANDMA. *She watches* NURSE *leave.* GRANDMA *is still for a moment. Mumbles. She is clueless without her nurse and*

---

44 For no reason.

is in shock from MALOBEE's *news. She sits. This is the first moment when the audience experiences* GRANDMA *alone. She is scared and appears small. Beat.*

GRANDMA   Nurse. Oh. Nurse. Where did you go... Shabnam. Come back, na...

Beat. She sits. Lights to next scene.

SCENE ELEVEN

MALOBEE standing still. She is narrating letters. Lights can indicate time change without drawing attention.

Letter 1

MALOBEE   I am sorry, Amma. I am. Please talk to me, Amma. I haven't heard your voice in a week. Ma refuses to tell me how you are. I don't know what to do. Please write back to this letter. Please forgive me, Amma.

Letter 2

Hope this letter finds you well. Ma said that you have a cough—are you feeling better? I am thinking of you all the time. Please write, Amma. Ma said that you are still so angry. I want you to know that I love you so much. Ma and Baba are getting to know Mark more. He is coming over more and things at home are better. Write to me?

Letter 3

It's my birthday today. I waited all day for your call. No card in the mail even. Amma, it is over seven months now.

Anyway, how is your time with Ma going? Is it good to see her after so long? She is saying that you look very thin. Why are you not eating? Did you like the gifts that I sent for you? Did Ma tell you stories about Mark? She really likes him now. Write to me?

Letter 4

I am graduating tomorrow Amma. We get to wear hats here and then throw them in the air. Mark and I are both celebrating after. Please send me your blessings. I spoke to nurse Shabnam yesterday. I knew you were sitting right there and listening. She is saying that your breathing is getting worse? Please take the medicine Ma sent for you. Feel better and write if you can.

Letter 5

Amma, I called you so many times today. Nurse Shabnam said that you didn't want to talk. I wanted to tell you this over the phone. Mark asked me to marry him, and I said yes! Please will you come to the wedding? Please will you bless me? Ma said that she will make all arrangements if you want to come. Please will you come? Please?

SCENE TWELVE

MALOBEE changes to GRANDMA. *Her breath is constrained.*

GRANDMA
My soul be hurting. My soul be hurting. All my life I be running from them.

NURSE
It's time for celebration, dadi. Stop crying like this, you will fall sick.

GRANDMA
Why? Why she is marrying this Muslim? Why they are infecting my family?

NURSE
Again you have started. Stop your Muslim talk today.

GRANDMA
Filth. Filth you all are. Do you hear me? You all deserve to die.

NURSE
Enough, na, dadi. Years after years I am hearing you saying about the dirty Muslim. You think we deserve it?

GRANDMA   Yes. Yes, you all deserved it. The gods be cursed you.

GRANDMA spits at NURSE.

NURSE is deeply insulted. She wipes the spit off her chin and looks at it. She speaks slowly and in a chilled tone.

NURSE   Yes, dadi. You are right. I am cursed. To be spending my days wiping the behind of a Hindu to feed my son. I am cursed. To watch my father be killed. By your people. Them asking, "Hindu ya Muslim?" "Hindu ya Muslim?" He told the truth. To watch my mother be thrown from a truck and my Ochin village be burned to the ground. How a little girl deserved that? You only tell me?

NURSE changes to GRANDMA. GRANDMA looks at Shabnam, trying to process the information. GRANDMA must appear weak and small. As if she is about to make peace with God before death. Slowly, she speaks after three beats.

GRANDMA   What? What village you say you are from?

Beat. Beat. Beat.

Ochin… Ochin…

Beat. Beat. Beat.

For my one mistake I am make the gods have brought this on me... Forgive me. Forgive me. Forgive.

Beat. Beat. Beat.

Dear Malobee, I am writing to you to ask for my forgiveness. I am making peace with the gods. And Allah. Forgive me, shona. I was angry. I have made mistakes... I am sending you my bangles. Wear them on your wedding day. To you and Mohammed.

Beat.

Blessings. Blessings. Blessings.

Beat. She takes four breaths and stops. She is dead.

SCENE THIRTEEN

GRANDMA changes to MALOBEE. She walks to her position from the start and picks up the unopened letter. She reads it. Beat. She discovers GRANDMA's gold bangles inside the envelope. She puts them on. Beat.

MALOBEE   I will remember this journey with you. The road beyond me is for me to discover... but I know this... and I know this because I truly believe that you will be travelling with me. Amma, I am leaving on my journey now. With you. With me.

Lights fade to black.

The End

ACKNOWLEDGEMENTS

My sincere thank you to Andy McKim, Hugh Neilson, and everyone at Theatre Passe Muraille; Annie Gibson, Blake Sproule, and everyone at Playwrights Canada Press; my family in India; Non; Peter Lewis; Aaron Armstrong; Barbara Lorainne Laing; Cathy Stasko; Dawn Nearing; Erika Batdorf; Gregory Danakas; Iris Turcott; Jessica Glanfield; Judith Thompson; Marie Dame; Paige Moore; Rachel Katz; Suzy Yim; Tammy Fox; Yvette Nolan; Andrew Cheng; Colin Rose; Judith Rudakoff; and Layne Coleman. Amma and Laxman Da—thank you for the inspiration.

Anusree Roy is a Governor General's Literary Award–nominated writer and actor whose work has toured nationally. Her plays include *Brothel # 9, Roshni, Letters to my Grandma,* and *Pyaasa.* Her opera librettos include *The Golden Boy* and *Noor over Afghan.* Her latest libretto, *Phoolan Devi,* will premiere in New York City in the fall of 2014. She holds a BA from York University and an MA from the University to Toronto, and is the co-artistic director of Theatre Jones Roy. Anusree is currently working on her first TYA play, *Sultans of the Street,* which will premiere at Young People's Theatre in the spring of 2014 and as a story editor and actor for the TV series *Remedy.*

MIX
Paper from
responsible sources
FSC® C100212